Copyright © 2020 by Aimee F. Rop

All rights reserved. No part of this book may be reproduced or used in any manner without permission of the copyright owner except for the quotations in a book review.

When I was almost 9 years old
I realized if I could become
any kind of artist, it would
mean everything to me.

I think it was the great joy
I felt each and every day,
when I used my many art supplies
in my own creative way.

I couldn't wait to share with Mom
all I wanted to do.
I hoped she would support me and
help make my dreams come true.

Mom said, "My sweet dear Clementine,
I know you have such a creative side.
I want you to do everything each day to let your imagination be your guide.
You can be a photographer, teacher, fashion designer, graphic designer, architect, . . .whatever your heart desires."

A huge smile came across my face,
with my Mom's words so true.
So I will begin this journey
of learning . . .

WHAT WOULD AN ARTIST DO?

I will learn about all of the great artists.

I will not be afraid to get messy.

I will visit museums and study art.

I will practice,
practice,
and practice some more.

I will get a different perspective.

I will explore new places and....

I will find friends like me.....

15 years later. . . .

TA-DA!!!!!!
My dreams came true!
I am an elementary art teacher......

"To all of the artists out there..
Never stop living life to the fullest
and following your dreams!"

~Aimee F. Rop

SPECIAL THANKS TO-

My sons, Adam and Connor-
You are my inspiration
and biggest blessing. You have
filled my life with pure joy.
I can't wait to see
where life will take you....
my favorite dreamers.

My parents, Mike and Irena-
You have supported me
beyond words in each
chapter of my journey.
Thank you for
being my biggest cheerleaders
and helping me see
my dreams come to life!

About the Author and Illustrator....

AIMEE F. ROP

I am an artist with lots of dreams even at a very early age. I was also blessed to have the support of lots of family and friends throughout my life to keep moving forward in doing what I love.

Just like Clementine, I am an Elementary art teacher for many future artists in Northern Virginia. I am also a mom to 2 active boys that keep me loving life's adventures.

For fun I am a photographer of people, animals, and nature. I love the color blue, cats, and dragonflies!!

My dream to be a writer and illustrator for a children's book has always been a goal for my passionate life. I hope you enjoyed Chementine's art journey to discover herself and her dreams as well!!

Keep on dreaming and living creatively! Each day gets you closer to who YOU want to be!!